88 Angels
Elizabeth Doreen Wilder

Photography by Rob Henderson
and Elizabeth D. Wilder

First published 2012 by D Publishing
This edition published 2020
Text copyright © Elizabeth Doreen Wilder 2012
Photographs copyright © Rob Henderson and Elizabeth Doreen Wilder 2012

ISBN:978-0-6487561-5-6

Silverbird Publishing
PO Box 72
Eltham Victoria 3095
www.workingtype.com.au/silverbird

Dedicated to Murray Barnes
'An angel among us'

Table of Contents

1	Acceptance	1
2	Accord	3
3	Achievement	5
4	Aesthetics	7
5	Affection	9
6	Ancestors	11
7	Approval	13
8	Aspiration	15
9	Attitude	17
10	Attraction	19
11	Bells	21
12	Beauty	23
13	Belonging	25
14	Betterment	27
15	Birth	29
16	Bliss	31
17	Breath	33
18	Brightness	35
19	Brilliance	37
20	Clarity	39

21	Comfort	41
22	Companionship	43
23	Contact	45
24	Courage	47
25	Dignity	49
26	Devotion	51
27	Dusk	53
28	Elements	55
29	Encouragement	57
30	Enlightenment	59
31	Expansion	61
32	Faith	63
33	Freedom	65
34	Generosity	67
35	Gentility	69
36	Giving	71
37	Goodness	73
38	Grace	75
39	Happiness	77
40	Humbleness	79
41	Humour	81
42	Influence	83
43	Innocence	85
44	Joy	87
45	Kindness	89
46	Knowledge	91
47	Liveliness	93
48	Loveliness	95
49	Magnificence	97
50	Maturity	99

51	Mirth	101
52	Music	103
53	Newness	105
54	Observation	107
55	Optimism	109
56	Outcomes	111
57	Patience	113
58	Peace	115
59	Pleasure	117
60	Prophesy	119
61	Protection	121
62	Purpose	123
63	Quality	125
64	Quietness	127
65	Rain	129
66	Refinement	131
67	Relief	133
68	Respectfulness	135
69	Reversibility	137
70	Safety	139
71	Security	141
72	Sensation	143
73	Sensibility	145
74	Sharing	147
75	Solitude	149
76	Starlight	151
77	Stillness	153
78	Surrender	155
79	Sweetness	157
80	Sympathy	159

81	Teaching	161
82	Tenacity	163
83	Thyself	165
84	Trust	167
85	Truth	169
86	Unwinding	171
87	Warmth	173
88	Wishes	175
Photographs		176

Introduction

How they came to me.
When I was a very little girl, I would stand squarely on our back veranda, which faced east and look out at the glorious clouds in the morning, afternoon, and anytime that I was on my way to the backyard to play. I would look up into the sky, and take in the enormous variety of clouds when they appeared. Being Melbourne, in Australia, which suffers from quite heavy rainfall, they appeared often. Even as a wee tot my mother would put me in the garden just by the coloured sweet peas along the fence planted lovingly by my father, who was an avid gardener. I loved it out there in a sixties bouncing baby basinet, I bounced away as I wobbled, my growing little legs getting stronger; until eventually I could walk, enjoying both the clouds and the mature coloured sweet peas, by then almost to the top of the fence providing a kaleidoscope of colour.

I remember looking up into the endless sky, and feeling that those clouds were places I could actually go to, and developed an urge to work out how to get there before I could speak.

Not really knowing that I'd just come from 'there' to get here, it became my earliest fantasy and my earliest ambition, before walking or talking those clouds had me fascinated! With their ever-changing moods and vacillating myriad of changes, my mind was hypnotised with their beauty and mystery.

I was certain, standing on that back veranda later as a four year old, when I could walk and run that the clouds were a place where you could walk and then keep walking, and even pick the most interesting ones to climb! This fantasy happily continued until I was around five years of age, and once able to speak took the conversation up with my mother. You see, I thought everyone could go there. My very practical, no nonsense mother straightened me out quickly to the fact of weather and wind and water and clouds and I never thought about them quite the same way again, until I found my Angels.

How I began to experience them.
The first experience that memory serves was while we were driving in a car in the sixties, and somehow we swung around a corner. I would have been

around six at the time, and I put my hand on what I thought instinctively was a handhold, which turned out to be the door handle of the car. If my Aunt, who was in the backseat with me, had not grabbed me when she did, I would have simply fallen out of the speeding car at an intersection with heavy traffic.

I remember seeing the bitumen of the road speeding in my view and being totally disoriented as to up or down momentarily. I know that there was a quiet invisible hand of help that time in saving me just before my Aunt grabbed me, from most certain injury or worse.

Prayers and prayer feedback came into play.

Once I became a little more familiar with their energy, I noticed my faith in them grow as a young woman, and quietly found myself doing, (perhaps as instructed) small rituals when I would hear of someone who was ill or going through some tribulation. One of these was to light a little tee-light candle for the person with their name written on a piece of paper at the top, the date, and the type of help needed. I would 'loan' them some of my Angels for a period to help them along and get through their difficulty.

To my astonishment this always worked. My faith grew rapidly in the small but very real service that any of us can do with something as simple as a candle and a prayer directing the energy of the Angels toward hardship. Anyone's!

This worked equally well on strangers as well as people I knew, and often I would receive feedback from friends on how well the people mentioned in these little prayers were either recovering or changed in circumstances fairly rapidly.

I kept going and still use this practise all the time, so part of this book is to share not only my experiences, but especially to give you the opportunity to use this book for sincere contact with your own. By working with your own Angels and the ones in this book, it is the intention of the author to bring to your life the faith you need to climb any of your own personal mountains (or clouds), in assisting others who may be having a little trouble looking up.

Quietude in soul.
Before you begin your connection with your own Angels, find a quiet place in your home. It is preferable that you eventually only use this space for your

quiet time to connect with yourself, God, Goddess, all that is. Whatever you believe in. No matter what way you experience it, this space is where you will go every day, or whenever you feel the need to 'connect' with Source.

Ritual of Candle Lighting
Have candles and something ready to light them with, ready. You can decorate this place with fresh flowers or a scented oil burner. I find rose oil a particular favourite of my Angels probably because it assists in opening the heart chakra to loves' presence. The scent of roses is also connected with Mary Magdalenes' energy.

You may wish to use Lavender, as this is a great space cleanser as well as providing you with a calming mood before you begin.

It is the intended by using the book that your own Angels will become familiar to you, and be of comfort to you when you or someone you know or care for, are in need of light.

There are no rules to working with your Angels, except for clarity of mind and a sincere heart. Your intention will always answer your guidance, so it is a very practical idea to be as centred about your intention as possible, and use visualisation to help you.

Visualisation
This is as simple as taking a few relaxing breaths to clear your mind, and emptying it of all thoughts, then visualising the intended person or the things you are blessing with your Angels' energy and then clearly sending that message from the heart. Imagine the person or thing done i.e. the healing already occurred and see the person smiling and without fear.

My most important experience of their Healing Powers.
The certainty of their existence in most branches of history is unprecedented, and it is my belief now, absolutely that they exist among us, around us, with us at all times with unfailing love, if only we could become more still and aware of their guidance and presence.

Recently, I went through a potentially fatal illness, and in my hospital ward one night my Angels appeared, singing an old favourite forties song of mine, swaying with my spirit, urging me to recover and restoring my soul.

That one visit strengthened me in a time of great need and some of the most difficult physical challenges I had ever faced.

The next day from the window of that same ward, a giant rainbow appeared in the sky, my verification that my angels and my clouds were still with me and urging me to have faith to move forward and past my illness by showing me the greatest healer of all – hope. Moreover - it worked. I did recover slowly, and gradually my spirit was restored and so my physical health to some form of quality of life. I know now and attribute this help to being open enough to sense my Angels rushing to my assistance with overwhelming Love to urge me on to recovery. They were indeed messengers.

When I first came through the worst of my therapy in hospital, my psychic vision had increased remarkably. I could also hear with greater clarity than ever, perhaps because I had not ever been this quiet in my entire life, which meant I was listening.

My vision around people was very clearly whatever colours were going on in their auric field, and let me tell you – some energies I witnessed were not what was what they presented physically.

These sharp definitions in auric fields and my sensitivities to them at the time were remarkably helpful in defining who may be the most productive visitors to have around at the time. When you are ill or in an extraordinarily weak physical state, I believe God gives you that extra sight to ensure you can recognise which energies you may want near you at the time. As many people feel energy (some more-so than others), it makes sense that when you are in a weakened state you need to be a little more cautious about what types of energies you may be able or unable to tolerate. You also absorb certain energies, and in a weakened physical state, your rate of absorption goes up. So definitely ensure that the energies are giving rather than borrowing your energies, which most people do subconsciously. Having done some metaphysics work, prior to my illness; over a period of 15 years really helped me help my Angels to make contact now most important to my own need for healing.

This work is indeed what I owe to them and the least I can do in gratitude of them having faith to restore me. It is with the greatest hope that by sharing these beautiful Angels with you or someone you love, that this hope is passed along in the same way all spirit experiences restoration.

May your own Angels bring you whatever you need at all times and introduce you to the loving Angels in your life, waiting only for your invitation to recognise their presence.

Good is God with an extra 'o'.

My belief is that all symbology, inclusive of the words you are reading now, are philosophically merely a chain of ideas forged over time and influence. From many languages, symbols and histories, which we absorb into our lives in accordance with our original tribal teachers, our parents, we then expand with our own experiences and cultures throughout the course of our lives.

Indeed, inside each of our cerebral cortex's are 100 trillion neural connectors at work at all times, especially so in the mystery of healing. With this great gift, we all have Angels. This appears to be just another sense to me, or anyone who has any Angelic experiences.

They are there, whether acknowledged or not, to guide, safeguard and help us discover the reason we are here.

So have a heart and an open mind as you enjoy these Angels, as they wish to transmit only Love to all, and to reconnect you with your own great Angels who have been watching over you all this time.

To me the word good is just God with an extra 'o'. When you take a moment to think of your associations with this word, you will notice a small but subtle shift in the way you feel. This is more than merely the power of positive thinking, it is a DNA strand that remembers the word and all its' associations throughout time. Indeed the word's origin is that of Godliness:

Godliness the condition or quality of being Godly
In my mind, we may as well have put an infinity sign between the g and the d, as it would accurately describe the symbology of moving ahead in the most prominently positive emotional landscape. Even Goodbye contains God perhaps seen as a later interpretation of 'God be with you', a very old saying still used today.

Most certainly we would all love God to be with us all the time. The fact is that he/she/all that is in the Universe is 'with' us all the time. We are the testimony of all our fathers' fathers and mothers' mothers' right back to the beginning of humanity on this planet, and even further back to star seed.

Therefore, whatever star seed you are made of, it makes sense that this travels 'with' you from lifetime to lifetime to lifetime, no matter what form your matter takes. It is my belief this part of us travels with our eternal soul.

The rest is up to us all to distinguish by our choices, and summoning the very best of our soul or spirit to ensure we live our lives to the fullest, with the wonderful vehicle called the body as an assistant vessel to attain our full spiritual growth.

So, with this understanding we all can be, no matter what the challenge or the difficulty, knowing that everything can change in the blink of an eye, better able to bless all that we are so fortunate to experience.

The people in our lives are the reflections of what we need to overcome or know within ourselves. They are our teachers. Understanding this, helps to 'know thyself' in a new light. A light filled with knowledge and curiosity with the fascination of all we are so fortunate to know of our lives in one short lifetime.

So from my own original star seed come my '88 Angels' to you, whoever you are, whatever your journey; may they remind you of your true worth in this vast Universe of all possibilities.

1
Acceptance

Resistance often is an invitation
For a visitation and salutation,
Give to me where you need to go
I'll alert all who need to know.
'I am the Angel of Acceptance'

2
Accord

Antipathy of soul
In seeming small or bold
A knowing calm
That soothes all is well with all
'I am the Angel of Accord'

4   88 ANGELS

3
Achievement

Tho' thou art strive
To be at thine best,
Your truth is always
Shared in help.
Your striving wins
By allowing my aide
'I am the Angel of Achievement'

4
Aesthetics

I see most beauty
In all things
Developed senses of
All creative delight
When you create anything
Touching heart and soul
I have visited your sight.
'I am the Angel of Aesthetics'

8   88 ANGELS

5
Affection

I pour upon the lonesome heart
And visit all who feel unloved
I sit with strangers
All the time
And whisper softly
From above.
'I am the Angel of Affection'

6
Ancestors

I have come with thee
On journey long
Longer than time
As you know of...
My secret is in you
And your children's sons
And your daughter's womb
From whence all have come
'I Am the Angel of Ancestors'

7
Approval

Although most think
In need of me
Or somebody's
To be met for more
This idea abandoned long ago
They left me here to tell you all.
'I am the Angel of Approval'

8
Aspiration

You have many of me
Contained in every soul
You dream in hope
Endeavours great
You keep me lively
All of Heaven is yours
You will need me to get to her gates.
'I am the Angel of Aspiration'

16   88 ANGELS

9
Attitude

Stay positive
Inside this view
For it may change
So do you grow
The more developed
Better handles all news
If overdone
The less you know.
'I am the Angel of Attitude'

10
Attraction

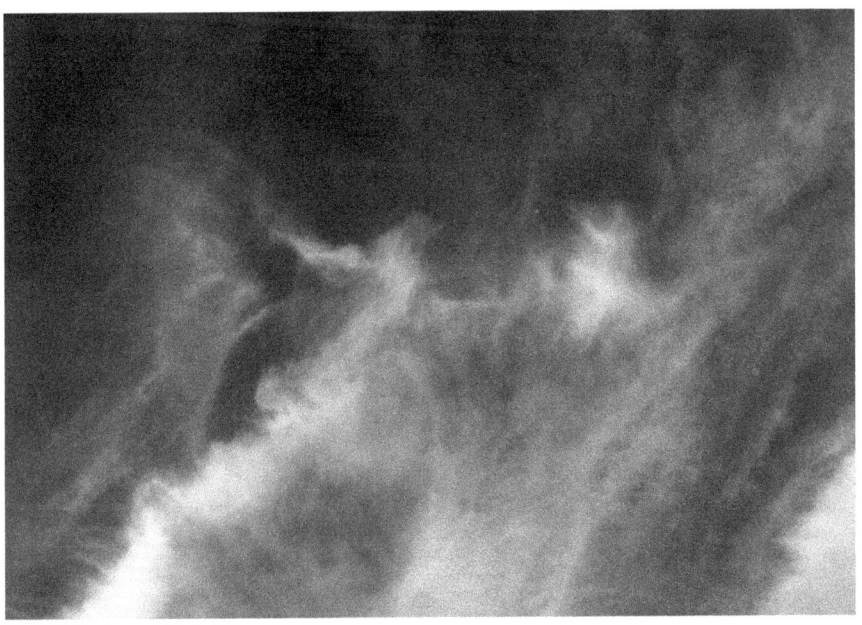

Like magnets in
Your central light
The source of whom
You will become
Is all of soul's knowledge one
Purest energy of attraction
'I am the Angel of Attraction'

11
Bells

My aural field
So light or loud
Ye hear me chime
Near you I play
Reminding sound of presence dear
To let you know
I am ever near...
'I am the Angel of Bells'

12
Beauty

In a blush of roses
My cheeks delight
In the art of ages,
Such things of right
Express her passage
In all you do
For she is thine
Who is also you!
'I am the Angel of Beauty'

13
Belonging

Gliding on the beams of love
I land gently as a dove
To tinker with your heart so strong -
To ensure my Dear you indeed belong!
At times so lonely
You feel you cannot bear –
Rest assured sweet child
I am always there!
'I am the Angel of Belonging'

14
Betterment

From all situations
I can spring to your aid
For this challenge is always
Within every way
Your job is to try me
And try me some more
Till your best is in sight
Then do better - some more...
'I am the Angel of Betterment'

15
Birth

This gift is thy treasure.
All manner of souls
Your true inner knowing
At birth is sown
Called the soul with a body
To accompany hence;
Until back to God you return
Once your lifework all blessed!
'I am the Angel of Birth'

16
Bliss

You may feel me calm upon
Your heart will open
As you feel my song
Then realise- not a thing amiss
'I am the Angel of all your Bliss'

17
Breath

You hold me in
You let me out
I am the one
Throughout your life
That gives you such hold upon
May you never be without me
'I am the Angel of Breath'

18
Brightness

Living in Stars
As bright as moons
My light is your shield
When darkness alludes
So fear not little children
Or big children too
Use my light in your mind
To guide and bless you
'I am the Angel of Brightness'

19
Brilliance

Be not unaware
Of your inner core
Of magnificence
And eternally more.
When you feel this light
Be gladly aware
Wherever you are
I am always there
'I am the Angel of Brilliance'

20
Clarity

As the crystal clear waters
I drop into flight
I am never away
From the purest in light
I will come with a flourish
A burst and a gust!
But belief in me
Is your birthright in trust.
'I am the Angel of Clarity'

21
Comfort

Settled softly on your pillow
Or your sofa or chair...
When you're relaxed and calm
Is when I'll be there.
I make you feel terrific
So snug and secure
Of my constant attention
You can always be sure...
'I am the Angel of Comfort'

22
Companionship

Wherever you've been,
At every turn,
In all circumstances,
Am I with you still?
I wait for instruction,
Of every sort,
My love for you eternal,
Forever with you in thought.
'I am the Angel of Companionship'

23
Contact

Do not fall sweet child
From Heaven's grasp
Belief in us
Is all that we ask
Keep us intervening
It's positively clear
That we'll stay with you always
We are forever near!
'I am the Angel of Contact'

24
Courage

Upon your feeble, I bestow
An extra spiritual knowledge
For fear is teacher
Of thyself to know
I am with you wherever you go.
'I am the Angel of Courage'

25
Dignity

Although we are with you
In your darkest hour
As strength overcomes all
Is our eternal vow
Building your life on this
One truth for all
Will see you avoid
Distaste for bliss
'I am the Angel of Dignity'

26
Devotion

There is no greater compliment
To a deities delight
Than to have my assistance
Whilst you pray at night
I am in every church
Upon every stone laid
It's my work in the making
That peace brings to the brave.
'I am the Angel of Devotion'

27
Dusk

When softness merges
From day to night
Iridescent hues
Last sparks of light
I come as quickly
As I gently go
So the day that has been
Is yours to know
'I am the Angel of Dusk'

28
Elements

Wind sings my song
Sun breathes my light
Water washes all sadness
Back to perfect light
Air gives you your breath
Whilst the clouds flutter by
As you enjoy my giving
These will all support time!
'I am the Angel of Elements'

29
Encouragement

We wait for those
In need of faith
With restoration
At our gates
Fear not your courage
As you forge ahead
Your brand new plans
Are destinies pledge!
'I am the Angel of Encouragement'

30
Enlightenment

Through shimmering mists
I take on all unknown
To you at this time
From whence you will grow
I pour into atmospheres
At blinding lights' speed
And from me your heart opens
At Gods' light heed!
'I am the Angel of Enlightenment'

31
Expansion

I am more than thy thoughts
I am part of all minds
To see me you must
Be willing to shine
I will fill all your senses
Within and without
Until you feel me clearly
Without any doubt!
'I am the Angel of Expansion'

32
Faith

In Heaven's arms
For you I wait,
Devotion I will rally
With confidence not late
Until you need me –
And trust you can,
I am part of every
Child, woman and man.
'I am the Angel of Faith'

33
Freedom

You are given me at birth
And never taken away
I am yours for the keeping
Upon every day
I live within hearts
With no need for regret
I am alpha omega
To all of Gods' tests!
'I am the Angel of Freedom'

34
Generosity

Open your heart
And give freely, you see
When you do simply this
You will see lots of me!
For the gift is but yours
So send it along
Your life will be boundless
Limitless and strong...
'I am the Angel of Generosity'

35
Gentility

Soft as feather down,
You'll glow always with this,
For its' understanding
Brings only bliss...
For the Lords and the Ladies
Are always bound
In this quality
They are truly crowned!
'I am the Angel of Gentility'

36
Giving

So easy to do
With as small as a smile
Igniting the heart
Of every child...
What you have
Is best shared
As is its' true worth
As you have been blessed with this
From others since birth...
So use me freely
And daily and often
As you watch the hardest
Of hearts, become softened....
'I am the Angel of Giving'

37
Goodness

From your heart to your head
Are you feeling me near?
I am joy everlasting
The ending of fear...
I am graced by your presence,
Seen always in delight,
With my joy right beside you,
Your future is bright!
'I am the Angel of Goodness'

38
Grace

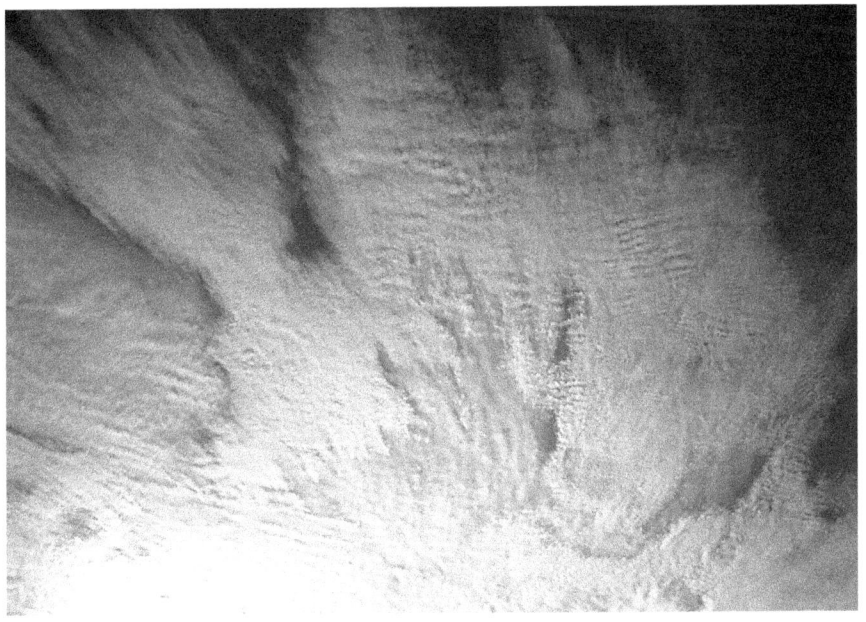

In church pews I await
Till your company's near,
To ensure that you feel me
When everything's clear.
Fear not! I don't leave you
And I won't hesitate
To be right there by your side
At Heaven's Gate!
'I am the Angel of Grace'

39
Happiness

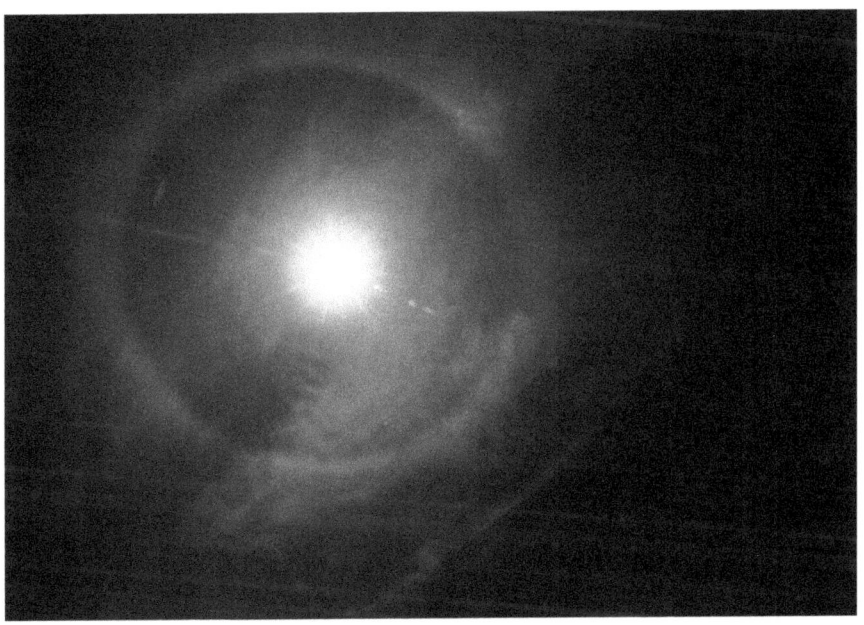

Bursting with sunlight,
I sing to you now,
And forever hold starlight
In this emotion – be showered!
I am simple in nature,
Look to birds and to trees
And within all their glory
You will see only me!
'I am the Angel of Happiness!'

40
Humbleness

I am counting my blessings
As God will know
All the gifts I'm so fortunate
To have – to grow
Blessed with dear friendships
And Love all around
For all that, I have
To grace – I am bound!
'I am the Angel of Humbleness'

41
Humour

When the blue days you think 'pon you
Turn around all your sorrow
You will feel me smile near you
Better looking tomorrows...
By a laugh or a gesture
I'll bring your smiles back
Get you onto the hilarity
Of life's endless track.
'I am the Angel of Humour'

88 ANGELS

42
Influence

Only I can offer,
Something unique and treasured
If you use it, you'll receive
More than your measure.
In social circles I wield,
My almighty sword,
In the light of pure goodness
Very close to the Lord!
'I am the Angel of Influence'

43
Innocence

Fear not that you keep me
Throughout your life
I make all an adventure
Without question or strife.
Lock me safe in your heart
Dear, sweet beautiful child
And I'll make your life safe
In mercy and mild!
'I am the Angel of Innocence'

44
Joy

You will feel me at random,
Where the oak meets the leaf,
On every grass blade
Under happy bare feet.
You are the vessel,
For the heart, we all read…
To show as much of me
Wherever there's need!
'I am the Angel of Joy'

45
Kindness

Be mindful of me
In your day-to-day life...
I am the message you give
When anyone's in strife!
Show me with gay abandon
Be random for sure...
For what you give of me
Will come back evermore...
'I am the Angel of Kindness'

46
Knowledge

You already know me
From eons, you contain.
To achieve me remember
You will n'er be the same...
Blessed minds will unravel
All my beautiful gifts,
As your time passes on
Through my essence you'll sift.
'I am the Angel of Knowledge'

47
Liveliness

I bathe you in sunlight
In Love's heavenly kiss
To show you through gratitude
There is nought that you've missed
I am all the Love
With me no further wondering
I'll leave you full of aliveness
And never left blundering!
'I am the Angel of Liveliness'

48
Loveliness

The smile that always greets you
You are heavenly to touch
Your heart warmed extension
Is felt in trust
Blossom sweetly, Dear child!
As I am ever near
Your soul is my entrance
My Love without tears!
'I am the Angel of Loveliness'

49
Magnificence

Hear me with wonder
Whenever you speak
Or play the piano
To its' ultimate peak!
I am the wonder of mountains
Of mystery too,
All knowledge is understanding
All waiting for you!
'I am the Angel of Magnificence'

50
Maturity

I will wait till you're older,
My gifts sweet to the ear
Bound in wisdom and gallantry,
With each meaning most clear.
With you right when you need me,
I am patient you see,
For I pass on to young ones
The very best of me...
'I am the Angel of Maturity'

51
Mirth

No sombre moods or grimaces
When my light descends
One and all
Are friends,
With gaiety's embrace
In sheer delight
Of everyone's laughter
Ringing day and night
'I am the Angel of Mirth'

52
Music

In the wind I play softly,
Birds love me even more,
For the tune that I give you –
Is one Universal chorus.
Swing jazz and thy classical,
All favourites of mine too.
With me you will go far
Not a tune you can't do!
I am the Angel of Music!

53
Newness

Presents await you
And everything's clear
You will delight and surprise
Whenever I am near
Think yourself as deserving
Upon every new day,
In the sunrise, awaken
As in all, I see 'play'!
'I am the Angel of Newness!

54
Observation

Watch closely sweet child,
With eyes like a hawk
Then you won't miss my messages
All before talk.
The beauty you'll see
But the eye of beholder
Every branch of the tree
And all things once you're older!
'I am the Angel of Observation'

55
Optimism

Look up and you'll see me,
Assisting your plight
I have mercy in abundance
Purity and light!
I keep all your goals going,
Keep the road ahead clear...
And whenever in doubt,
You will feel me most near!
'I am the Angel of Optimism'

56
Outcomes

Just flow with the process.
In this all will be found,
For you know not the future
Until the present is ground!
All ambition is folly
When you're not right here, now.
For only in this time
Will all possibility be shown.
So be not caught in tomorrow
It will still surely come,
Have precious faith in the present
Where all knowledge - is one.
'I am the Angel of Outcomes'

57
Patience

She waits with such strength
Known to all that survey
Her courage is plenty
Upon every day
She smiles at the go-getters
Amused by their rush
For in me she holds fortitude
Ability and trust
'I am the Angel of Patience'

58
Peace

The attraction is in you
To bring me ever near
For the joy and the love
Are all yours my Dear!
I am evermore with you
In that place you must look
Whether bird softly singing
Or babbling brook!
'I am the Angel of Peace'

59
Pleasure

The tinkling of rain
On the rooftop you hear
Is a sign as you smile
That I am everly here...
Roses, hats and new dresses
Favourite shoes, lollypops...
Fruit in ravenous abundance
Peculiar snowdrops...
'I am the Angel of Pleasure'

60
Prophesy

In Nostradamas I flowed
As in all of you hearts
When connected to mind
You make a great start
Look to me for your knowledge,
Of where your life goes,
Keep in mind I'm a follower
Of all things that grow!
'I am the Angel of Prophesy'

61
Protection

Although there are corners
Where darkness exists
I light them all up
With my heavenly bliss!
Fear not all you wanderers,
Of corners of Earth
I will ensure you no loneliness
With the presence of mirth.
'I am the Angel of Protection'

62
Purpose

I give you the ability
To harness what you see,
To a million horses
To carry thee to me...
When you need to be steadfast,
Stay ready and strong,
And in the blink of an eye
You will hear my sweet song!
'I am the Angel of Purpose'

63
Quality

A Heaven of laughter
Or theatre, or dance
All your favourites right here
If you'll spare me a glance.
Using me, you'll use less
But ensure all the way
That only the best
Is for you every day!
'I am the Angel of Quality'

64
Quietness

As bird of prey,
Sit quiet 'pon branch,
I watch ever with them
Before their next dance.
In that moment before,
Any flap of their wing
I jump into their hearts –
And cause them to sing!
'I am the Angel of Quietness'

65
Rain

I look so like a snowdrop
On glass tables collect...
To the trees and the plant – life
I am thirst truly met.
I bubble in streams
And ripple through rivers
My droplets expand
Eternally givers!
'Pon your pond I will visit
Sometimes more than a day
It's my true delight
Everywhere that I play...
'I am the Angel of Rain'

66
Refinement

Take your thoughts
Into heights –
Vibrant echoes
Of beauty....
Nought but the best
For your jewels
And your duty...
True to the finest...
Spent flowers not to your taste
You must be with me now
Make Heavenly haste...
'I am the Angel of Refinement'

67
Relief

I will take away shadows
And whispers galore...
Monsters under the bed
And silence darkness the more...
When illness strikes
I will take it away,
To bring back the sun
On the gloomiest days...
I live to remove fears –
And worries adjusted
Where you go I'll be with you
I am simply a must!
'I am the Angel of Relief'

68
Respectfulness

Where courtesy is shown
In good deeds and good manners,
It is right there you'll find me
Polite homage my banner.
To all that you know,
Even enemies dire,
Find me irresistible,
For my meaning is higher!
So show me with civility
Cultivation and polish,
To your friends, family and children,
You'll assure I'm acknowledged!
'I am the Angel of Respectfulness'

69
Reversibility

It may. It may not.
It's a fickle affair
And I'm in every one
In the this - that way chair.
Listen closely to the Universe
And you'll pick where I am
My visits surprise and release –
Sometimes even banish.
If you have any difficulties
You will need me My Dear!
Just keep shifting the Universe
And Voila! I'll appear!
'I am the Angel of Reversibility'

70
Safety

Rest thy wings
Little Angel!
Over your soul
I keep watch...
Although all
May appear troubled,
I am with you
When lost.
Let not a furrow
Or wrinkle appear,
For within any sorrow
I am ever near!
'I am the Angel of Safety'

71
Security

I'll secure that door
And check all the locks
Are good for your soul
And all of your lot.
In crowds I'll be there,
Ever close to your back,
I am ever in contact
I have a real knack!
'I am the Angel of Security'

72
Sensation

Feel the touch of a feather,
Or bubbles bursting on cheek,
I am made for your pleasure,
It is I that you seek
While you're eating or drinking
I am here with you. Trust!
That my essence is glory
And an absolute must!
'I am the Angel of Sensation'

73
Sensibility

Keep your head clear
Whenever I'm round
I'll be putting in work
On you staying safe and sound.
When the world seems bizarre,
Of frightfully unknown,
I'll be there right beside you
With good sense all known!
'I am the Angel of Sensibility'

74
Sharing

You can have plenty of mine
If I can have some of yours
The more you do this
You'll experience more joy
It is fitting and proper
To daily do this
As your gift has much more
Meaningful bliss!
'I am the Angel of Sharing'

75
Solitude

When serenity surrounds thee,
Peace, comfort and care...
I am present to feelings
It's when I am there!
When all noise has subsided
And stillness abounds...
That's the time I am usually
Making my rounds...
So be still and enjoy, Indeed acquiesce,
For my visits are part
Of all you've been blessed!
'I am the Angel of Solitude'

76
Starlight

As I sparkle above you
I sparkle within
For in eons gone by
At beginning of all things
I dance with you in the Universe,
And all you survey,
I am the being in all things
You will see today!
'I am the Angel of Starlight'

77
Stillness

As you calm every breath,
So you see me in this –
In your Lotus flower moments
I give you utter bliss
I cannot be contained
For you must practise my Dear,
To find all the truths
I'll show you when near.
'I am the Angel of Stillness'

78
Surrender

When you give in to me,
I only give back.
For with all my powers
I will give you the facts.
You need me to guide you,
Through hard times and good,
And believing in me,
Is a habit you should.
'I am the Angel of Surrender'

79
Sweetness

The distant gaze
Of the rose in bloom
The total stranger
Walking into a room.
The Loving eyes
Of a mother to child
In these Dear things
You find I will hide.
'I am the Angel of Sweetness'

80
Sympathy

When all is in pain
I will comfort your need
With my swift understanding
And courage indeed!
There are always my helpers
There is always some cheer
As you're comforted gently
To safety my Dear!
'I am the Angel of Sympathy'

81
Teaching

When learning the numbers
Or letters as well,
You'll find me in your pen
To ensure you spell.
I am an over enthusiast
Never enough of me seen
For you'll always be using me,
Even when you have been!
'I am the Angel of Teaching'

82
Tenacity

You will find that you need me,
So elegant once known...
As I auger success
In all you've been shown.
Oh, mirror me when,
You feel the times' tough...
And I'll reveal you're blessings
As diamonds in the rough!
'I am the Angel of Tenacity'

83
Thyself

I am rivers' end
And the trickle of stream
Floribunda abound
With very bright beams
I will shine on your heartstrings
Forever aglow
I am the Angel of Angels
You already know!
'I am the Angel of Thyself'

84
Trust

Put your faith in me totally,
For the ebb and the flow,
With the grounding of me...
You will surely grow.
Effective in making
Creativity abounds...
Learning me gives you wisdom,
Love, purity abounds!
'I am the Angel of Trust'

85
Truth

Forthwith you will see,
I give you what you know
You will see right through things
If you use me to grow.
Seek me ever and always
For I am knowledge of all
If you use me for good
I'll show you even more
'I am the Angel of Truth'

86
Unwinding

Sit back, relax...
And soon you will feel
My loving warmth
Seep head to heel...
Take the time to enjoy,
Meditate on me...
For my secret is yours
To your best, I will heed!
'I am the Angel of Unwinding'

87
Warmth

In the arms of a cuddle
You'll feel me aglow,
When you sit by the fire,
It is me that you'll know!
When the extra soft blanket
Is lovingly placed
For your comfort and ease
Keeps you in my embrace!
'I am the Angel of Warmth'

88
Wishes

Your wish is granted
Just by thinking, you ask?
And we will make blissful
Work of the task
We wait for your requests
But we have to be asked!
Please include us at the beginning
Don't leave us until last.
'I am the Angel of Wishes'

Photographs

By Rob Henderson:
Chapters 1,4,5,6,7,8,9,10,11,12,13,14,15,16,17,18,19, 20,21,22,23,24,25,26,29,30,31,32,33,34,35,37, 39,40,42,43,44,45,46,47,48,50,51,53,54,55,56, 57,58,59,60,61,62,63,64,65,67,68,69,71,73,74, 77,78,80,81,82,83,85,86,87

By Elizabeth Doreen Wilder:
Chapters 2,3,8,27,28,36,38,41,49,52,66,70,72,75,76,79,84,88

www.ingramcontent.com/pod-product-compliance
Lightning Source LLC
Chambersburg PA
CBHW051537010526
44107CB00064B/2756